GETTING MORE OF YOUR PEOPLE DOING MORE OF THE THINGS YOU WANT THEM TO DO MORE OF THE TIME

MARK WATSON

First published in Great Britain in 2004

Published by Ted Publishing
Waltham House
5-7 St. Mary's Terrace
Mill Lane
Guildford
Surrey
GU1 3TZ

British Library Cataloguing in Publication Data.
A catalogue record for this book is available
from the British Library.

ISBN 0 9549083 0 9

Printed in Great Britain by Butler and Tanner.

GETTING MORE OF YOUR PEOPLE DOING MORE OF THE THINGS YOU WANT THEM TO DO MORE OF THE TIME

MARK WATSON

01

IT'S HARD,

GET OVER

If you truly want to engage and align people in your business, expect to experience frustration, friendship, anger, disbelief, enjoyment, a sense of being let down, passion, and a lack of praise and recognition.

EXPECT TO CHANGE THE WAY YOU WORK, TO SPEND MORE TIME TALKING TO PEOPLE, TO LEARN MORE ABOUT HOW TO BRING ABOUT ENGAGEMENT. EXPECT TO IMPROVE YOUR SELF-AWARENESS, AND TO DEVELOP YOUR WIDER EMOTIONAL INTELLIGENCE. EXPECT YOUR LIFE TO CHANGE FOR THE BETTER.

Do not commission your HR people and expect them to do it for you. Get personally involved, and if this jars with you, get your act together!

MOST OF WHAT YOU

02

NEED YOU ALREADY HAVE

In many organisations the people with the real know-how are the people who are doing the work, relating to customers and colleagues and making direct use of the company's resources in the frontline. The issue is, how do you inspire people with the confidence to use and share their know-how in ways that will build value in the company?

WHAT DESTROYS CONFIDENCE IS WHEN COMPANIES BRING IN SO-CALLED CONTENT EXPERTS TO TELL PEOPLE WHAT TO DO, BUT NOT HOW TO DO IT. COMPANIES WOULD BE BETTER ADVISED TO SPEND THEIR TIME AND RESOURCE HELPING THEIR PEOPLE PUT INTO PRACTICE THINGS THEY ALREADY KNOW.

I came across a good example of this in a large retail organisation with over 100,000 employees working in their stores. Having spent millions of pounds with external 'specialists' on customer service, they found the best ideas that could be practically implemented came from a competition they ran for store colleagues. The competition generated hundreds of stories, each citing practical examples of great service. They also found that the motivation was much higher to implement ideas that had come from colleagues rather than consultants. The company went on to invest resource in helping colleagues share their ideas and supporting them with guidance on how to put them into practice.

Do you know more about your customers than your...

PEOPLE?

3

If you understand more about your customers then you will be better equipped to sell them more of your products and services. Seems sensible, and indeed companies are spending billions doing this.

The thing is, to maximise the potential of knowledge about customers we need to engage our people to be able to do the right things. And to do that we should understand who our people are, what they need and want, and how they feel. Yet, I remain dumbstruck by the lack of understanding that companies have of the people who work there.

We talk about relationships and customer relationship management, but I wonder how good are your managers' relationships with their people? If you want your people to be relating to your customers, shouldn't your managers be relating to your people? It is, of course, impossible to form a good relationship with another person if you don't know anything about them.

How many of your managers know about the interests, aspirations and life goals of the people who work in their teams? How many of them make judgements about their people based on mechanical processes and theoretical scoring systems?

ALL YOU NEED IS

L♥VE

4

During a recent conversation with a high profile Chief Executive of a large technology company, I asked him what he thought his biggest challenge was in continuing to build his business. His response was, "I need to bring more love into the company".

Afterwards, I reflected on what a simple and confident answer this was, but how alien it would be to many other Chief Executives. But think about it, how powerful would that be in your organisation and how powerful would it be as an opening to provoke a dialogue with your executive team?

PEOPLE SAY,

> ## *"IMPROVE COMMUNICATIONS!"*

WHAT DO THEY REALLY MEAN?

05

It seems to be a short-hand for many different things such as:

- not being told what to do
- not knowing everything that is going on
- frustration over the boss' behaviour
- no opportunity to talk about the company with colleagues
- lack of involvement in decision-making
- feelings of being uncared for and undervalued
- a lack of understanding of what the company stands for
- an absence of clear direction
- a feeling that no-one listens
- a feeling of being patronised
- too many emails
- too many separate pieces of information

and so on and so on…

But these are not situations that can be eased simply by providing more information. In most organisations people are already drowning in information. What they are crying out for is context and an understanding of how to organise and relate this to what is more important and what is less important in achieving their goals.

Today, communication is as much about the behaviour of those communicating and the interaction that is necessary with people as it is about the content. However, common practice is still based on a reliance on hierarchy and a belief that once the information is out there, people have been communicated with.

Organisations now have access to many more media and devices for communication, although in most cases we are abusing the opportunities provided by simply asking the new media to do the work of the old. The truth is that all organisations now need a strategy for 'communicating' that goes way beyond sending information, and that is a rigorous and robust part of the business planning process.

How has your strategy on communications radically changed in the last three years?

06

Everything is connected to everything else

Change one thing in a company and everything else changes in some way. But just look at the way many organisations go about involving their people. It's done in a way that implies that things happen in a compartmentalised and separated way. Little wonder that employees complain of hundreds of pieces of apparently unconnected information, often caused by the fact that the information is prepared by people working in isolation to achieve their own specific and personal objectives.

Why do middle managers complain of 'initiativitis', lots of different initiatives, each apparently a stand-alone, each very important and each requiring a chunk of their time? People are left asking questions such as: Which initiative is more important? Which piece of information will help me make the most impact on what we are trying to achieve? How does all this fit together?

We know it should all fit together. But how much emphasis are we placing on making sure there is a common purpose and a shared understanding of that, and a very obvious common thread that ties everything together?

STOP ALL TRAINING!

IF YOU WANT YOUR PEOPLE TO LEARN THINGS THAT WILL BENEFIT THE COMPANY, AND LET'S HOPE THEMSELVES ALSO, THEN STOP SENDING THEM ON TRAINING COURSES.

I STILL HEAR PEOPLE COMMENTING ON WHAT A GOOD COURSE THEY HAVE JUST BEEN ON AND WHAT THEY HAVE LEARNT BUT WHAT A SHAME IT WAS THEY WERE UNABLE TO PRACTICALLY APPLY ANY OF IT WHEN THEY RETURNED TO WORK. DID THEY REALLY LEARN?

CLOSELY EXAMINE THE OPPORTUNITIES YOU CREATE FOR PEOPLE TO LEARN. TO WHAT EXTENT IS YOUR COMPANY STILL RELYING ON SENDING PEOPLE ON TRAINING COURSES TO ACQUIRE NEW PRACTICAL SKILLS? MAYBE THIS IS OK TO LEARN ABOUT SOFTWARE OR PURE SCIENCE. IT'S NOT OK WHERE PEOPLE NEED TO LEARN ABOUT LEADERSHIP, TEAM WORKING, RELATIONSHIPS OR OPERATIONAL MANAGEMENT.

HAVE THE IMAGINATION AND SHOW THE LEADERSHIP AND CONFIDENCE TO GIVE PEOPLE ASSIGNMENTS IN THE REAL WORLD THAT WILL GIVE THEM THE PRACTICAL EXPERIENCE THEY NEED TO BRING OUT AND DEVELOP THEIR TALENT. AND MAKE SURE THEY'RE SUPPORTED WITH THE RESOURCES TO BE ABLE TO FULFIL THEIR ASSIGNMENTS.

THEN, TAKE TIME TO GIVE THE INDIVIDUAL FEEDBACK ON WHAT WAS GOOD, AND HOW IT COULD HAVE BEEN BETTER.

"IN THEORY, THERE IS NO DIFFERENCE BETWEEN THEORY AND PRACTICE. IN PRACTICE, THERE IS."

ONCE
IS NEVER
ENOUGH

In most walks of life and in most situations, learning something requires several iterations and a fair amount of practice, something which we all have experience of from the earliest days of learning to walk through to playing a musical instrument, or mastering a piece of software.

ALTHOUGH WE KNOW THIS, WHEN WE MOVE INTO A CORPORATE SITUATION WE SEEM TO FORGET. WHAT I MEAN IS MANY ORGANISATIONS BELIEVE THAT THEY CAN PUT THEIR PURPOSE AND STRATEGY ACROSS THROUGH A ONE-OFF COMMUNICATION. I HEAR, "WE TOLD THEM THAT AT THE CONFERENCE LAST YEAR" OR "I GAVE A PRESENTATION ON THAT ONLY LAST MONTH" OR "WE PUT THAT IN WRITING AND SENT IT TO EVERYONE SO THEY MUST KNOW".

In reality, these instances are simply an introduction to an issue or a plan. The challenge is to think of what needs to be put in place to create the opportunities to practice and reinforce the point.

As a leader, you need to put more energy and time into reaffirming what your people most need to know. And if this feels like you are repeating yourself, then that is good – it's your job!

"The faster I fail, the faster I succeed." If your people are afraid of making mistakes, then they will not feel confident to take the risks that are necessary to change the status quo and your people will not learn as fast as they could. Learning only comes through experience. Learning how to ride a bike in theory is a whole lot different to learning through actually riding.

If you place the emphasis on learning from mistakes, rather than punishing mistakes, then progress is made. The challenge for leaders is to suppress the reflex that focuses on why the mistake was made rather than how to put things right and how to avoid the same mistake again. Another pitfall is for the leader to behave in a way that indicates a belief that, given half a chance, people will behave in a wreckless, uncaring manner leading to continuous errors and mistakes.

There is also a challenge for the individuals who make a mistake and how they handle it within themselves. People are often much harder at punishing themselves against an expectation that they should not make mistakes and even that they are stupid for making them.

The opposite of this is an inability to listen to critical feedback (blind arrogance) and a refusal to confront one's own behaviour through rationalising feedback in a way that explains the 'mistake' away.

How do you learn from your mistakes?

9. FORCE PEOPLE TO MAKE

MAKE IT
CLEAR
WHAT
COUNTS

{10}

You wouldn't play your heart out for a sports team if you got in the dressing room at the end of the match and didn't know what the final score was. Or worse still, you've been playing football and someone tells you the score is 135 runs for four wickets. Seems obvious.

Why then do we expect people in our organisations to play their hearts out without giving them the score in a way that they can relate to? People need to know what counts. That might mean something very simple such as knowing what questions to ask customers, or what actions they need to take to earn their bonus. It rarely means how shareholder value has been increased.

YOU MAY HAVE A VERY WELL DEVELOPED AND CLEARLY THOUGHT THROUGH STRATEGY FOR YOUR ORGANISATION, OR YOU MAY ONLY HAVE A FRAGMENTED SENSE OF HOW YOUR ORGANISATION SHOULD BE IN THE FUTURE. EITHER WAY, WE SHOULD ALWAYS REMIND OURSELVES THAT HUMAN BEINGS SPONTANEOUSLY LOOK FOR THE WHOLE STORY. OUR BRAINS ARE WIRED THAT WAY.

HENCE, A GOOD STRATEGY MIGHT NEVER COME TO FRUITION BECAUSE THE COMPLETE PICTURE WAS NEVER MADE AVAILABLE IN A WAY PEOPLE COULD UNDERSTAND. THEY GOT SO FAR AND THEN MADE UP THE REST. LIKEWISE, THE FRAGMENTED SENSE OF DIRECTION NEEDS TO BE WORKED ON BY THOSE WHO LEAD THE ORGANISATION UNTIL THERE IS A SHARED UNDERSTANDING. OTHERWISE, EACH LEADER WILL BE COMMUNICATING THEIR OWN INDIVIDUALLY COMPLETED STORY TO THEIR PEOPLE.

If people only
have part of the story...

...they will
make up
the
rest

eleven

Why CEOs need to know how people learn

Number Twelve

An organisation's only sustainable competitive advantage is its ability to learn faster than its competitors.

Markets have become more competitive, customers more demanding, pressures on costs ever greater, the need to do things faster more and more pressing, and competitive advantage often hangs on the ability of the company to adapt and turn on a pinhead.

Whether it's the launch of a new product or service, the implementation of a new system or process, or building relationships with existing and new customers – all depend on people's ability to learn new things.

So, if you don't know how people learn, you won't be able to take direct action to make it more effective and faster. If you do know, you will be able to challenge and replace many out-of-date practices in order to sharpen your company's competitive edge.

Go and find out, and start by understanding how you learn.

THIRTEEN

YOU GET WHAT YOU GIVE

Expect people to behave in a way that reflects the way you treat them. Try to think of this beyond how you might personally relate to people and take a look at things from the perspective of someone who works in your company.

What do they see on a daily basis? What does it feel like when they walk into the building? What are the ways in which they get the information to do their jobs? What does it feel like in their place of work? What sort of food does the restaurant serve? What kind of commercial restaurant does it most resemble?

Listen to your managers and the way they talk about the people in the organisation; and find out what the word on the street is about the people who are leading it.

This will tell you why people are behaving as they are in your organisation. If you want to change that, work on changing people's experience, and then, over time, people will change their behaviour.

P.S. IF YOU GET TO THE POINT WHERE YOU FEEL YOU ARE GIVING A LOT BUT NOT GETTING MUCH IN RETURN, THEN YOU MAY HAVE THE WRONG PEOPLE.

WED	THU	FRI	SAT	SUN
	01	02	03	0
07	08	09	10	1
14	15	16	17	
21	22	23	24	
28	29	30	31	

Make an appointment with yourself

Awareness of self goes hand in hand with awareness of others. What differentiates the effectiveness of one leader over another often comes down to their level of self-awareness. Further, it is now understood that qualities reflected in an individual's emotional intelligence play a dominant role in leading and engaging people. Where are you at? How do you feel when answering questions like these?

If you don't understand yourself how can you understand others?

What are your life goals and how were they shaped and formed?

What are your values?

How are you intelligent?

How do you learn?

How do others see you?

How are you aiming to build better relationships with others?

COSTS
ARE
GOOD

15.

IF AN ORGANISATION HAS NO COSTS THERE IS NO ORGANISATION.

THE REAL ISSUE IS TO USE YOUR COSTS WHERE THEY WILL DO MOST GOOD.

MANY ORGANISATIONS IN RECENT TIMES HAVE BEEN USING TOO MUCH COST TO MAKE THEIR PRODUCTS OR DELIVER THEIR SERVICES. STRIPPING COSTS HAS CREATED A COST CONSCIOUS CULTURE WITH ARGUABLY MORE EMPHASIS ON THE COST THAN THE VALUE.

THE REAL CHALLENGE IS TO ENABLE YOUR PEOPLE TO SEE AND UNDERSTAND HOW TO CREATE VALUE USING THE ORGANISATION'S COSTS AND HOW TO ELIMINATE COST THAT IS NOT INVOLVED IN BUILDING VALUE.

CREATING AND BUILDING THINGS IS A VERY ATTRACTIVE PROPOSITION TO MOST PEOPLE. THEY BECOME INTRIGUED AND INVOLVED, AND GROW A SENSE OF PRIDE. THE MODERN ROLE OF FINANCE IN ORGANISATIONS IS TO ENABLE PEOPLE TO TAKE PART IN THIS.

You can't change

16

someone else's
behaviour

"You can lead a horse to water but you can't make it drink." Equally, in the workplace of today, you can give someone a job, ask them to achieve something, or change their role description, but you can't force them to change their behaviour.

Everybody chooses how they feel, be it up beat, down beat, positive, or cynical. If you want people to behave in line with a values set or a promise made by the company to customers, then create the conditions where people have the opportunity to decide how they need to behave.

VALUES

Every organisation has values, whether or not they are captured in some form of values statement.

THE VALUES ARE ALMOST ALWAYS A REFLECTION OF THE BEHAVIOUR OF THE PEOPLE WHO LEAD OR HAVE LED THE COMPANY.

Employees are used to, and tired of, the drill. They've seen it all before, where a set of words are put forward to describe the values. They know how to play the game of memorising these words so that they can perform like seals when asked by management what the company's values are. They remain bemused by managers who seem satisfied by those who can recite the words and damning of those who can't remember the words but nonetheless make good contributions to the company.

VALUE FROM

If you want to impact the values then first look at your own behaviour and that of your colleagues in the executive team. How self-aware are you and your colleagues? How well do you know each other? How much time have you spent talking about values as a group? How good are you at enhancing the value of your organisation by bringing values to the fore and using them to differentiate your organisation from its competitors?

Statements don't count. Values exist only through the behaviour you demonstrate.

PEOPLE WHO ➡ BLAME THEIR LIVES ON OTHERS

18.

Beware! We all choose how we feel, although to listen to people talk in some companies it's as if their problems are someone else's fault. Arguably one of the biggest challenges of leadership today is to promote, encourage and inspire the confidence in people to take responsibility for themselves; to learn how to confront themselves and the issues in their working lives; to take responsibility for their own learning and to behave as equals. How much feedback do you get that points out problems and tells you how difficult you are making things?

ENSURE THAT PEOPLE HAVE THE FACTS AND UNDERSTAND THE CONTEXT, SO THEY HAVE NO CHOICE BUT TO TAKE RESPONSIBILITY.

Communicate
with
your
ears

We all know how boring it is to go on a date with someone who spends the entire evening talking about themselves, asks no questions and when you speak talks over you.

Leaders have lots to say about their organisations and sometimes about themselves too. The leader's challenge is to avoid the mindset of "I need to tell them what they need to know". They also need to demonstrate interest – if a leader fakes interest their communication style quite often becomes patronising and everybody has a super-sensitive radar for that.

When you listen and engage in conversation you demonstrate interest and respect for people. It is also the time when people learn most about you and most about what the company is trying to achieve.

The golden rule is two ears, one mouth – use them in that proportion.

20

Young and old, experienced and inexperienced, senior and junior, general manager and specialist, administrator and professional, functional people and operational people, people just starting out and people about to retire, front office people and back office people, men and women.

Companies that exploit the diversity within their organisations tend to thrive.

Great things happen when people can meet and swap stories, share things with each other without prejudice and without agenda.

Go out of your way to create opportunities for people to mix in this way.

Move it from the 'nice to do' list to the 'must do' list.

Don't be a remote control boss

How, where, and when do you have conversations with your people? Are they at your request and set up as meetings with the boss? Or are they spontaneous, informal and on a drop-in basis? Are you protected by your team around you from having to talk to people? Do you actively avoid, for whatever reason, situations where people can just pop in or come along or stop you to talk? Do you receive most of your information about what's on people's minds through surveys and reports from other managers?

To be a great boss today you need to enjoy people and enjoy talking to them without patronising them or behaving in a defensive, aloof manner. You've got to know what it's like to work alongside them, know what they experience first-hand when they deal with your customers, eat and drink with them, and allow them to gain first-hand experience of what's on your mind and what you value.

If you behave like this, the word will spread like wild fire. If you don't, people will second guess you and what is said about you around the company will resemble the garbage written about celebrities in the tabloid press.

Where do you eat your lunch?

Get in amongst the people in most organisations and you'll find examples of where people feel they have been patronised by the leaders of the company: through what was written in the newsletter, what was said and the way it was delivered at the conference, or just the way I was spoken to in the elevator this morning.

22

What follows in this environment is reciprocal behaviour from the people in the company. It's just as patronising to second guess the CEO or to assume a leader has time to read your 16 page report that has no summary or business justification and to take the piss behind a leader's back whilst at the same time demanding a large bonus.

And what about that job application? Were the two lines written by the applicant an adequate summary of their life? But who's to blame? Is it the applicant because they just used the two lines on the application form or is it the company for issuing such a ludicrous document?

People are interesting, but only if we behave in an interested way.

WHO'S PATRONISING WHO?

23

WHERE THE PAY DIRT IS

Even though few leaders would disagree that differentiation, competitive advantage and success are driven by the company's ability to harness the knowledge and know-how of its people, there still seems to be an obsession with machine-like features when it comes to upping the performance of the organisation.

People have never responded like machines and they never will. And although they can respond and adapt to frameworks and instructions more suited to machines, they will always be compromising their true potential.

If we are to maximise the potential of our people we need to look to more humanistic approaches. There is an abundance of evidence and ideas in the natural world. This is where the real pay dirt lies if you are looking to improve the performance of your people.

You might just be better off spending a day talking to a zoologist than getting advice from a performance management advisor.

24

Too many of us take ourselves too seriously. Too many of us get hung up on the things that we can count in our organisations. We're driven by the tangible, structured, systemised and process-ridden aspects of our organisations, supposedly running them ever more efficiently and making more and more decisions based on our well-informed evidence.

So what about play, humour, relaxation, sport, music, the things that we naturally choose to do or seek? Why is it that these seem ever more consigned to the parts of our lives that are not involved with work? As leaders, if we're not having fun our organisations cannot be fun places to work.

Fun has the power to unlock the potential of many people. View it as a frivolous potentially wasteful thing, and you will be wasting your people's natural talents.

25

FITTER PEOPLE PERFORM BETTER

Yet, so few approaches to performance management embrace the fitness of people.

With improved fitness comes greater confidence, improved ability to positively impact relationships, sharper decision-making and higher energy levels to keep pace with and enjoy a busy life.

The performance of any organisation is dependent on the performance of its people.

How people eat, how they move, their posture, state of mind and energy levels all have a direct impact on their performance.

Would your performance improve if you were fitter? How about the performance of the people in your organisation?

What will you do? What would your shareholders expect?

26. Drink lots of water

People don't
function at
their best
when they
are even the
slightest bit
dehydrated.
A 2% level of
dehydration
can lead to a 20%
reduction in brain
performance.

Competitive edge
comes from those who
are maximising their
performance, not just
playing a good game.

It's not that you don't
perform when you're
dehydrated, but how
much better your
performance
becomes when
you drink
enough
water.

27

The menu is not the meal

Starter

Menus in restaurants create expectations about the food
we are going to eat. We judge the restaurant by the experience
of eating. Fancy food prepared and served badly is a much
worse experience than simple food prepared and served well.

Main

Sadly, many companies spend a lot of effort preparing their
menu but fail to create an experience that matches. Think
about the values statement in your company. If your aspiration
is to serve 'fancy food', then the experience must live up
to the expectation you create.

Dessert

In short, if you must have a values statement, make it
very clear if it is aspirational, or be very sure it describes
how things currently are. Better to have something simple
and effective than fanciful and alienating. Better still, avoid
the values statement; concentrate on the experience and let
people tell you what it's like to work in your company.

Coffee

Menus and their associated experience obviously go
beyond the issue of values, but the same principles
will apply. Take good care!

28

YOUR
TOILETS
SPEAK
VOLUMES

How do you feel when you walk into a dirty, smelly toilet?

How do you feel when you walk into a spotlessly clean, fresh smelling toilet?

You can tell a huge amount about the culture and values of an organisation simply by checking out their toilets. Why is it that some organisations have spotless facilities whereas others have dirty, unhygienic ones?

If you're a CEO, how do the toilets you use compare to the toilets used throughout the organisation? And how do all these compare to the toilets adjacent to your reception?

Who's responsible for creating this experience?

Cynicism is a corrosive behaviour that can potentially destroy an organisation.

We are all cynical from time to time. However, we cannot afford to let cynicism dominate. And we must not run our organisations in response to cynical people and their destructive ways.

You can never win an argument with a cynic; the challenge is to expose the cynics for what they really are by creating a simple and undisputable picture of the truth. If you don't bullshit and don't try to hide or blur things, then there's nowhere for the cynics to go – they end up looking foolish.

GARLIC FOR VAMPIRES – UNDISPUTABLE TRUTH FOR CYNICS

30.

THE ONLY RESOURCE THAT INCREASES WHEN YOU SHARE IT...

If I have a tonne of steel and you have a tonne of steel, and I give you my tonne of steel and you give me your tonne of steel, we each still have a tonne of steel.

If I have an idea and you have an idea, and I share my idea with you and you share your idea with me, we now both have two ideas.

The good news is that each of us would use the other's idea in a different way to that which had originally been conceived, therefore making the return potentially much greater.

Knowledge is the only resource that grows when it is shared.

How are your people incentivised and rewarded for sharing their ideas?

31

EVERYBODY DOESN'T LEARN LIKE YOU DO

The pitfall for the leader is assuming that the best way to communicate is to put things across in a way that they find easiest to understand.

There are at least eight different human intelligences and everyone has them. Each of us has a different balance of these intelligences, meaning that we learn best in ways that suit our personal mix.

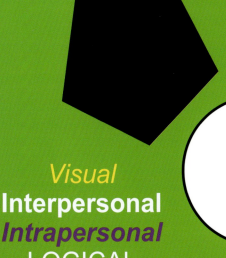

Visual
Interpersonal
Intrapersonal
LOGICAL
Naturalist
Linguistic
Musical
PHYSICAL

Therefore, the question we need to ask is not "Are you intelligent?" but, "How are you intelligent?"

Two intelligences (linguistic and logical) dominate in our organisations, the way we work.

The challenge for the modern organisation is to make sure that they present what they need to get across in a number of different ways to ensure they give themselves the best chance of reaching as many people as possible.

I once heard a film-maker being interviewed about his marvellous talent for film-making. He was asked, "Do people understand your films?" His reply says it all: "I know what I am doing when I tell a story through film, but I have learnt over the years that the many millions of people who watch my films find their own meaning and will often explain in graphic detail how my films tell stories that I've never even dreamt of."

That's fine when we're talking about entertainment. It's not fine when we're expecting people to take specific action as a result of the stories leaders tell about their organisations.

32
WHAT'S SENT

WHAT'S RECEIVED

ARE TWO DIFFERENT THINGS

Leaders can fall into the trap of using jargon terms and code that has meaning to them but has little relevance or place in the language of other people.

Be very ashamed of yourself if you hear yourself saying, "I've told them, so they should know". Next time you want to get something across, start by standing in the shoes of the people you want to reach and understand what's important to them and the language they use.

In short, get over yourself. It's the audience that is important, not you. And always check what people have received.

Drawing your own conclusions beats the hell out of being told what to do

Our brains are naturally wired to work things out for ourselves. When people tell us things we spontaneously check what we've heard against our existing knowledge and experience and then seek to check the information we have received and fit it within an overall context, a bigger picture.

If we sign up for the armed forces, part of the deal is suppressing this natural tendency. We quite simply have to follow instructions and orders – that's the way it is. Early industrial organisations were based on the military – it was clear to the leadership what had to be done and the easiest way to get it done was to tell people what they should do and hold them accountable for following instructions.

In today's environment, it is much less clear what needs to be done and it changes on an hour-by-hour, day-by-day basis depending on customers' changing expectations, new technologies and competitive challenges from just about anywhere. We need our people to be equipped to respond without relying on or waiting for instructions. The job of leadership has moved from knowing what to tell people to do, to ensuring people know what needs to be achieved. Then making sure people are supported with good information, tools and resources to get the job done in a way that maximises value for the organisation.

34

memorising the future

Our brains continuously prepare us to be able to cope with the future. Our subconscious mind runs through many different possibilities of what might happen to us and in doing so prepares us to be able to cope with whatever may come our way.

Sports people work on improving their performance through envisioning how they will beat their opponent, play the perfect round of golf or drive the fastest lap. They do this not because they are odd but because they are harnessing some of their brain's natural ability. In business, some organisations use scenario planning to ready their executives to deal with a largely unpredictable future business climate.

Most organisations are dependent on their ability to respond rapidly to changing customer demands and market conditions. This puts pressure on the ability of their people to adapt quickly. Harnessing people's natural ability to prepare for a range of possible futures can only improve this ability.

35

Are you emotionally committed to what you are doing?

If you're leading a company or responsible for leading part of a company, and you are not emotionally committed, do not expect your people to be committed.

CEOs and business leaders who read from the autocue or speak with language contrived by PR are becoming less and less credible to the people they need to engage and inspire.

People know when their leaders believe in and are committed to what they say. They listen to more than the rhetoric and hear more than corporate words.

36

DON'T SAY YOU ARE HONEST
BE HONEST

People say they value and respect honesty in their leaders and leaders say they value and respect honesty in the people who work in their organisations.

ALWAYS REMEMBER THAT WE CAN USUALLY SENSE HONESTY IN OTHERS. WE KNOW WHEN SOMEONE IS BEING STRAIGHT AND WE KNOW WHEN PEOPLE LIE TO US. WE KNOW EVEN IF IT REMAINS IN OUR SUBCONSCIOUS. WHEN WE HEAR PEOPLE SAYING THEY ARE HONEST WE WONDER... THE SENSE OF HONESTY IS ONLY CREATED THROUGH BEHAVING IN AN HONEST WAY.

No matter how you are challenged never be tempted to proclaim your honesty as a means to justify yourself... it stinks and sends the opposite message!

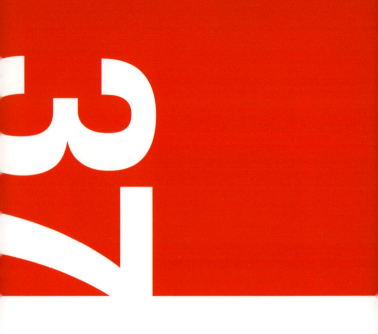

37

FOOLS

EMPOWERMEN

The theory of empowerment is admirable. Sadly, the reality can be somewhat different. I have seen many cases of people being caught in the jet wash of empowerment where the intention was positive but the effect destroyed confidence and left people confused and wondering what they should do.

Empowerment is great for those who can demonstrate they know what to do. But for others, structures and clear guidelines are more appropriate and certainly more effective.

Empowerment within a clear framework is positive. But the open use of the term can lead to some people seizing upon it and using it as a stick to beat top management. If you are drawn to use the word, make sure you define exactly what you mean by it in the context of your organisation and the people within it.

You want to build value in your organisation. You want to achieve the goals and performance targets that enable you to move towards your vision.

How much time do you spend listening to and working with the people that share your passion? Compare this to the amount of time and energy you spend responding to cynical people who are not aligned to what you want to achieve. Most of the time they shout the loudest in an attempt to draw more of your attention to them and away from working on achieving your goals.

You may be surprised by the answer.

For example, be careful about the messages you send through your people policies. W. Edwards Deming said you could tell a lot about an organisation by looking at the policy manual and checking the length of the policy on bereavement. The vast majority of people when they have a family bereavement just want some space to get on with sorting things out; their requirements are very simple and individual. What message does it therefore send if the bereavement policy is several pages long? Who did the organisation have in mind when this policy was written?

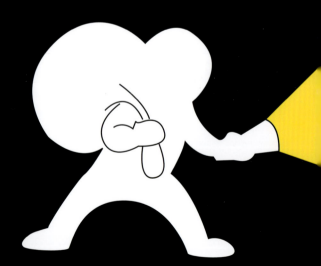

who's stealing

(38)

your energy?

WHICH
COUNTS
MOST...

Are the systems and processes of
your organisation supporting your
people to achieve their goals, or do
people feel there is more emphasis
on them becoming slaves to the
systems and processes?

39

...SYSTEMS & PROCESSES OR PEOPLE?

A quest for greater efficiency and effectiveness has led to a proliferation of new systems and processes. Huge amounts of resource have been justified and allocated to their creation, whilst investment in human performance has remained relatively unchanged.

Some businesses have lost their way, putting their faith in the system and process route towards a sustainable future, with their people just acting like modern-day mill workers.

Perhaps it's easier to work on systems and processes than to address the only source of differentiation – people.

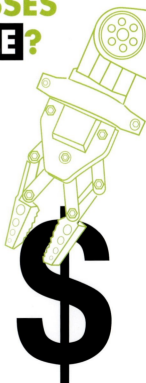

why are you having the meeting

Before we had access
to modern communication
channels, meetings were
often held to communicate
information, to brief people
on progress and news,
and to make decisions.

**Why do you need to hold meetings
in your organisation today? Are
you sure that you are only doing
what you can do in a meeting, or
are you doing things that could
now be taken care of in another
way? Are you maximising the value
of having a group of people in the
same room at the same time? Are
your meetings based on dialogue
and sharing ideas and experiences,
or are they based on detailed,
structured and packed agendas
that don't seem to respect the
talent that is in the room?**

When did you last plan
a meeting by thinking
about the diversity and
needs of the people who
are attending rather than
the agenda and what
needed to be got across?

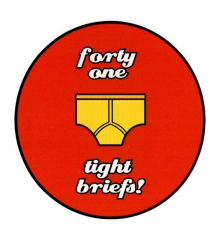

The quality of the brief often determines the quality of the approach taken to engage people in what needs to be done or achieved. This is a particularly challenging area for senior management, who are often clear in their own minds what it is they want, but fall down in the briefing they give to those they have charged with putting it across to others.

A simple approach to making things clear is to draw up two lists – one that is entitled "what it is" and one that is entitled "what it isn't". This forces the owner of the brief to be clear-cut about what they want and avoids misinterpretation by others.

Poor content is poor content no matter how you communicate it.

There are many situations where poorly thought through ideas and strategies are put across with great enthusiasm and at times great expense using sophisticated media and special effects. Poor content badly communicated makes no real difference – confusion reigns. Poor content well communicated destroys the credibility of those who conceived the content and at times can lead to the implementation of the wrong thing.

"THE BEST WAY TO DESTROY AN ORGANISATION IS TO IMPLEMENT A BAD STRATEGY WELL."

YOU
CAN'T
MAKE A
POOR
CASE
INTO A
GOOD
ONE

YOU
CAN
MAKE A
GOOD
CASE
INTO A
POOR
ONE

42

The situation where good content is poorly communicated is rather depressing, since people don't receive the message and potential is lost. Executives should spend the same amount of time working out how to get their ideas and strategies across as they do in formulating them.

Internal communication is vital. How strategic is it in your organisation? Do you have your best executives working on it? If not, why not?!

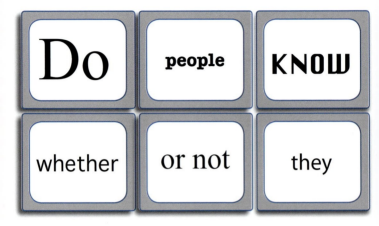

Do people **KNOW** whether or not they

Many of the people you employ support sports teams. They know who plays for their team, in what position and what their strengths are. They know about the other teams they compete with and what their comparative strengths and weaknesses are. They know the track record of their team, what they are aiming to achieve this year, how well they are doing, and what their chances of success are.

{ 4

3 }

They understand the club's heritage and what the club stands for, its values and how it is different from other clubs. Many will be able to quote endless statistics about this and previous seasons' performances, and more…

Do these same people talk about the company they work for in equivalent terms? Do they have the information and understanding to enable them to do so? What if they did? Is it reasonable to expect them to buy in to the company without this information?

People are naturally creative.

Why isn't your

44

business?

Nothing stifles creativity like conformity, regulation, and an autocratic command to follow instructions. People are naturally creative, but when forced to behave in a regimented way or forced to operate in an environment driven by fear, this creativity is squeezed out of them.

We all have the ability to be creative, and in many different ways. What we need is the space and confidence to practise what we are naturally good at. So, if you want your business to be more creative (and make sure you understand what that means before you make claims or put it in your values statement), take a close look at what is stopping people and get it the hell out of the way.

It's sad, but we live in a time when natural curiosity and spontaneity have been forced out of many people. Our work places are dull and dominated by processes and systems, and to some extent are responsible for removing this natural instinct. People know what to expect and that's good, or is it?

Only when things become interesting over a sustained period do people start to rediscover their curiosity. It could be argued that the fastest way to stimulate people's curiosity is to stop suppressing it. In this age we suppress people's natural behaviours and instincts at our peril.

We are some way off, but what if we could make it a requirement in our organisations for people to be themselves, and create conditions that allow them to be?

...DO YOU THINK
OF PEOPLE WHO
CAN'T READ?

I once witnessed a senior executive from a large corporation give a keynote presentation to an audience of several hundred people, all of whom worked for the corporation. Some were fresh graduates, some had recently joined from other organisations, others were veterans of more than two decades; all levels of seniority were represented in the audience. It was a competent enough speech that had the audience's attention without really setting them on fire. One short part really stuck in my mind. That was when the executive announced to the audience that he didn't use the internet and saw little point in logging on.

Later, I met with the same executive and asked him what he thought of people who could not read. He looked at me, puzzled by my question. Eventually, after a bit of prompting, he said he would see such a person as uneducated, and when prompted further, said that he would be extremely unlikely to hire the person to work in his team.

I then asked him what a bright, young graduate would think of an executive who announced to people they lead that they had never logged on to the internet.

46

47
Superstitious learning

More things went out of date today than they did yesterday or the day before or the day before that…

What worked in the past won't necessarily work in the future. What works in one set of circumstances isn't necessarily transferable to another. If we persist in teaching through case studies, we run the risk of equipping people with a bunch of stuff that used to work but is no longer relevant.

A significant challenge for top executives is to unlearn much of what they have learnt about business and how to go about engaging and aligning their people. They are under pressure to open themselves up to learn new things. Top executives should be the ones who are learning the most, most quickly.

Readiness
for the future

forty-eight

When people think about the future, they will usually project a smooth and direct progression from the present. Of course if we look back in time it's obvious that, certainly in the last century, that has not been the case.

A technique that can be very useful in preparing your people to face the future, implement a new strategy, or take a new direction, is to engage them in a dialogue on the organisation's history and how it has changed over the years, reviewing various important milestones, so that they can trace the change pattern and see that things did not happen in a smooth, steady way. Then as a second part of this dialogue, engage your people in talking about the current reality and what's in play in the organisation now. Then finally, flowing straight from this two-part dialogue, ask them to consider what issues, challenges and opportunities there will be for the organisation in the future.

The results can be quite amazing in terms of opening people's view of the future – vital if you want to involve people in the organisation's strategy.

I can't tell you how

There is no formula, no recipe, no process, no system that can be universally applied to engaging and aligning people. The truth is, every organisation is unique and completely individual because it is made up of different and unique people. Each individual organisation must draw on its collective confidence to work on its own approach that suits the time, stage in development, market conditions, offer, ability of its people and so on.

BENCHMARKING IN CERTAIN CIRCUMSTANCES CAN BE USEFUL FOR SPARKING IDEAS OR PERHAPS LEARNING ABOUT THE SYSTEMS AND PROCESSES AVAILABLE. AS W. EDWARDS DEMING ONCE ASKED, "WHY ARE SO MANY COMPANIES TRYING TO BE DIFFERENT BY BEING THE SAME?".

Take confidence in your wonderful, unique organisation and work out what you need to do to maximise its potential. And then if you need some help getting more of your people doing more of the things you want them to do more of the time, seek it based on how to achieve what you want to achieve.

IS THE CUSTOMER WILLING TO PAY FOR WHAT YOU ARE DOING RIGHT

NOW?

50

This is one of the best challenges I have come across in business. Try setting it for some of the areas you are concerned about in your organisation.

Perhaps you could even ask this question: **"Why** is the customer willing to pay for what you are doing right now?"